HENRY FC

A Life from Beginning to End

Copyright © 2017 by Hourly History

All rights reserved.

Table of Contents

Introduction
The Rise of Industrial America
Henry Ford's Early Years
Ford's Love for Engines
The Ford Motor Company and the Model T
Ford's Expansion into Everyday Life
Ventures in Later Life
Disdain of Labor Unions
The Anti-Semite Problem
Later Years and Death
Henry Ford's Legacy
Conclusion

Introduction

Of all of the industrialists who made life miraculously easier at the turn of the twentieth century, Henry Ford is no doubt one of the most famous. Just about everyone has heard of him and might recall that he was the one to introduce the assembly line into production, thereby making it possible to mass-produce practically everything.

There was nothing fancy about the names Ford used for his brand new inventions; but the Model T is instantly recognized as the car best known, even over a century after its creation. His Ford Motor Company would revolutionize the way business is conducted. Finally, not just cars, but many staples of everyday life, were being made affordable for the average person.

Not only were his factories innovative, but Ford introduced a living wage, something much touted in the news these days. His $5 a day wage was equivalent to $120 today. Everyone wanted to work for Henry Ford, and that too was part of his magic.

For it was a magical time in America and all across the Western world. New inventions, some re-worked from medieval times were suddenly being used far and wide. In addition to men being able to find viable jobs, women and minorities were also given consideration by Henry Ford.

But for all of his goodness, there was an anti-Semitic streak which would haunt him all of his days. It may have come from beliefs emanating from his childhood, and always resided in the background.

To his credit, Henry Ford is one of America's most celebrated industrialists. There is much to know about Henry Ford. So, grab a coffee and a seat and let's have at it.

Chapter One
The Rise of Industrial America

"Don't be afraid to give up the good to go for the great."

—John D. Rockefeller

The last quarter of the nineteenth century, those years from 1877-1900 are what is known as the rise of industrial America. One could say it all began in 1869 when the first transcontinental railroad was joined together at Promontory Summit, Utah on May 10. For the first time ever, America was now joined coast to coast.

Then by January 1870, John D. Rockefeller created his Standard Oil Company in Ohio. During that decade, over 2.8 million immigrants landed in the United States, most of them from Europe.

In October 1871, a massive fire destroyed the city of Chicago over the period of two days. Whether the inferno was started by Mrs. O'Leary's cow knocking over a lantern, was never determined. In any case, over 17,000 buildings were destroyed, leaving over 100,000 people homeless. Once Chicago started rebuilding, it would transform itself into a major industrial and economic center.

In 1872, portions of Montana and Wyoming territories were declared the Yellowstone National Park. This meant that people from all over could enjoy the splendors of the land.

That same year, it was learned that members of Congress had been involved in corruption. The Union Pacific Railroad company had been hired to build part of the transcontinental railroad. Instead of hiring outside contractors, Thomas Durant, the VP of Union Pacific, along with many stockholders created their own construction company, Credit Mobilier. By awarding the building contract to themselves, they reaped in massive profits.

Durant gave Union Pacific stock to many members of Congress who had been instrumental in helping with railroad legislation. Eventually, Union Pacific stock was declared worthless, and eleven members of Congress were accused of accepting it, thereby contributing to the railway industry corruption.

In St. Louis, Missouri a ring of distillers and federal officials were found to have been involved in tax evasion. Many of those indicted for the scandal were appointees of President Grant.

By 1876, Alexander Graham Bell patented the telephone. The Battle of Little Bighorn took place in June of that year, where General George Custer and his 7th Cavalry were massacred by Sioux and Cheyenne warriors. As settlers pushed west, there were increasing hostilities between them and the Native Americans. The Nez Perce Indians were pursued by the U.S. Army until they were finally relocated from Montana to Kansas and Oklahoma.

In 1877 railroad workers in West Virginia, went on strike to protest low wages and living conditions. The strike lasted more than a month, and there was violence which was halted by federal troops. People were beginning to rise up in protest.

By 1879, Henry George's *Progress and Poverty* was published. It dealt with the changing cycles of the industrial economy. Then all through the 1880s, drought and bad winters had devastated cattle herds in the West.

In July 1881, President Garfield was shot by an assailant, and he died two months later, in September. He was succeeded by Chester A. Arthur.

The following year, the Chinese Exclusion Act was the nation's first law to ban immigration by race or nationality. This prohibition would stay in place until 1943, and it prevented the Chinese from becoming Americans.

Also in 1882, John D. Rockefeller created Standard Oil Trust. The trust was formed to allow Rockefeller and his stockholders to get around state laws prohibiting one company from owning stock in another.

In 1883, the Pendleton Act was passed. This was an attempt to curb corruption and patronage. It introduced federal exams and merit requirements for the hiring of civil servants. In September, the Northern Pacific Railroad was at last completed. There was a "golden spike" ceremony at Gold Creek, Montana.

In 1884, Grover Cleveland was elected president. Long before modern-day presidents with their sometimes seemly baggage, Cleveland, a Democrat, was supported by many Republicans. He had been a staunch promoter of anti-corruption and had opposed Tammany Hall while being governor of New York. They were the Democratic Party political machine which controlled politics in New York City and throughout the state.

Cleveland was thought to be a shoe-in until it was discovered that he had fathered a child out of wedlock, had placed that child in an orphanage and the mother in an insane asylum. Yet most people didn't seem to care and voted for him to be president, anyway.

In 1886, anarchists gathered in Chicago's Haymarket Square to protest the police killing of labor strikers. Someone threw a bomb into the crowd, and when it was all over, eight policemen and several protesters had been killed. By December the American Federation of Labor was formed to organize skilled workers.

In 1887 Nikolai Tesla perfected alternating current which made it possible for electricity to be everywhere. Congress also passed the Interstate Commerce Act after receiving considerable pressure from small businesses and farmers.

By 1890 Benjamin Riis' book, *How the Other Half Lives*, documented living conditions among immigrants to New York City. The census of that year showed that immigrants now made up 14.7% of the population. Congress also passed the Sherman Anti-Trust Act, to prohibit trusts and prevent monopolies.

Just like today, the problem of tariffs was on everyone's minds back in 1890. Democrats said tariffs raised prices and enriched only the wealthy. Republicans argued that tariffs helped small businesses, raised workers' wages, and helped them combat low-wage competition.

By this time, America had the most factories and raw materials, sophisticated marketing and a very efficient distribution system that European markets couldn't compete with. In October, the McKinley Tariff was passed. It increased tariff rates, and it provided for reciprocal trade agreements. The tariff would prove to be very unpopular with American consumers and labor.

In December, U.S. troops slaughtered Sioux women and children at Wounded Knee Creek South Dakota. It would be the last battle to be fought for Native Americans. In 1891, Hawaii was annexed to the United States. Hawaii would not become a state until August 1959.

In January 1892, Ellis Island was opened. For the next sixty years until 1954 over 12 million immigrants to the United States would be welcomed here. In June, because of falling steel prices, the general manager of Andrew

Carnegie's steel plant in Homestead, PA, cut workers' wages and attempted to put down the union.

Frick promptly closed the mills and wouldn't negotiate with the union. Workers declared a strike and sought to contact Carnegie, but he made himself unavailable. Frick hired a private army to break up the strikers. The Pennsylvania State Militia was called in to stop the violence. The strike leaders were blacklisted, and Carnegie had now successfully broken unions in Homestead and all throughout steel country.

In 1892, Grover Cleveland was once again elected president, thanks to a third-party movement called the Populists. By the mid-1890s an economic depression would settle over the country and his second term would be a disaster. Cleveland sought to keep the country on the gold standard and tried to enact an income tax, which would be deemed unconstitutional by the Supreme Court.

In 1893, the Great Northern Railway was completed. The stock market crashed leading to the bankrupting of the United States Treasury. At the same time, unemployment increased. By 1894, workers for the Pullman train cars went on strike. This caused a stoppage all throughout Chicago rail lines and with railroads all across the country. The violence and prolonged strike marked the end of the American Railway Union.

In May 1896, the Supreme Court ruled on *Plessy v. Ferguson*, which held that Louisiana train cars could be segregated based on the constitutional doctrine of "separate, but equal." There were separate facilities for hotel rooms, drinking fountains, schools, going to the movies, riding a bus and buying a home. The Civil Rights Act of 1964 would end all that.

William McKinley became president in 1896 and two years later, and America would enter the war in 1898. Once they defeated Spain, America acquired Cuba along with

Puerto Rico, the Philippines, and Guam. With Teddy Roosevelt as his running mate, McKinley was re-elected in 1900. In 1901, J.P. Morgan would merge several of his companies with Andrew Carnegie's to form U.S. Steel.

Later in 1901, President McKinley was assassinated and died eight days later. He was succeeded by Theodore Roosevelt.

Between steel, railroads, shipping and modern inventions such as the telegraph, the telephone, and electricity, America was poised to reap the greatest rewards yet; that of the automobile and how it would transform the country and the world.

These years would be instrumental in getting Henry Ford's dreams off the ground.

Chapter Two

Henry Ford's Early Years

"Logic will get you from A to B. Imagination will take you everywhere."

—Albert Einstein

In the midst of America's Civil War, Henry Ford was born on July 30, 1863. His family lived on a farm in Greenfield Township, Michigan. Ford's father William had been born in Ireland to a family who was originally from England, and his mother Mary was born in Michigan to Belgian immigrants.

Henry Ford was the oldest of five children; soon there was Margaret born in 1867, Jane in 1868, William in 1871, and Robert in 1873. In his early years, Ford never thought of leaving his home place. Work was long and hard on the farm, and he always imagined himself staying there. The ranch was sizeable, and the family enjoyed a typical middle-class life, as comfortable as it could be.

For all of the hard labor involved in the running of a farm, young Henry believed there must be a better way. He would gather metal pieces and fashion them into tools, and this is where his love for mechanics sprung. When in his early teens, his father gave him a pocket watch, all Henry did was take it apart and put it back together over and over. By the time he was 15, Henry was disassembling and reassembling timepieces from friends and neighbors. He did it so well that people thought he was a watch repairman.

In 1876, Ford's mother, Mary, died suddenly. Feeling devastated, he had no liking for farming from that moment on. He recalled how "I never had any particular love for the farm, it was the mother on the farm I loved."

As a 16-year-old, Henry left home to start his first job. He went to Detroit and worked as an apprentice machinist for James F. Flower & Bros. Ford learned all there was to learn as a trainee and he worked studiously at his craft. After three years, he returned home to help his father run the farm.

During this time, Henry discovered that although he didn't love farming for its own sake, he was fond of tinkering with all of the farm equipment. He became an expert at operating the Westinghouse portable steam engine. Because of this knowledge, Ford was later hired by Westinghouse to service their steam engines. Along with his job, the resourceful Ford began studying bookkeeping at Goldsmith, Bryant & Stratton Business College in Detroit.

Henry Ford immersed himself with working and studying until 1888 when he met Clara Jane Bryant. They were married on April 11 that same year. An only child, Edsel, was born in 1893. The Fords enjoyed a long life together, and on the occasion of their fiftieth wedding anniversary, Ford was asked how he was so successful in marriage. He quickly and simply responded, "Success in marriage is the same as success in the car business: stick to one model."

By the time of his marriage, Henry Ford was becoming more religious. In his twenties, he walked four miles one-way to an Episcopalian church every Sunday. As is common with many young people, the young Henry was searching for meaning in his life; how doing great things could be centered in life but have a spiritual dimension to it as well.

By the time he was 26, Ford had accepted the concept of reincarnation which made more sense to him than anything the Episcopalians were talking about. Rather than walk away from his Episcopal faith, Ford just incorporated reincarnation into it.

About the topic, Ford stated that "Religion, like everything else, is a thing that should be kept working. I see no use in spending a great deal of time learning about heaven and hell. In my opinion, a man makes his own heaven and hell and carries it around with him. Both of them are states of mind."

It would turn out to be one of the things he loved to do best in his life; share his philosophies with the willing public. That, and build an affordable automobile. Both of these ideologies would come to define him as time went by.

Chapter Three
Ford's Love for Engines

"Don't find fault, find a remedy."

—Henry Ford

By the year 1891, Ford became an engineer with the Edison Illuminating Company. Two years later he was promoted to chief engineer. Lucky for him, by this time there was ample money and hours left over for him to begin working on his personal experiments on the gasoline engine.

In between working and providing for his young family, Ford was able to devote many hours to improving his machines and engines. It was in 1896 that Ford completed his first automobile. It was a self-propelled vehicle, which he called the Ford Quadricycle. Though not the first person to invent something like this, Ford made his self-propelled machine small enough and adaptable enough for the average citizen. He did his first test run of the Quadricycle on June 4 of that year.

By 1896, Ford attended a meeting with Edison executives where he also had the pleasure of greeting Thomas Edison himself. The Wizard of Menlo Park was very taken with Ford's automobile experimentations. Because of the extra attention being paid to him by Edison, Ford conceived and built a second vehicle in 1898.

By this time there were others interested in Ford's designs. With the backing of Detroit lumber baron William H. Murphy, Ford was able to resign from the Edison

Company, and he founded the Detroit Automobile Company on August 5, 1899.

As his vehicles started taking shape, Ford realized that they were of a lesser quality than what he envisioned and they were also at a higher price than what he desired. Unfortunately, Ford's first automobile company didn't last. It ended up producing only 20 trucks, and the business was dissolved in January 1901.

Up to this point, all Ford had created and designed was the result of long hours and an attitude of never-give-up. He passionately believed that no one ever makes mistakes, and he felt that everyone is put on earth for a purpose. It is your life's work to figure out what that purpose is. Mistakes, according to Ford, were more like the stepping-stones of life.

Still, his company was closed. Some people would just walk away, discouraged and never seek to take the plunge again. But not Henry Ford. With the help of C. Harold Wills, who would go on to be one of the first employees of the Ford Motor Company, Ford designed and built a 26-horsepower automobile in October 1901. He raced this car along with others in a head-to-head, and no one came close to being as fast.

Because of this success, Ford's former backer William Murphy and other stockholders formed the Henry Ford Company in November 1901 with Henry Ford as chief engineer. Although he didn't own the company, Ford was happy with the position he was in.

The following year, Murphy brought in Henry M. Leland as a consultant. By this time, Leland was almost 60 years old and knew a lot about engineering and precision machining. Once this happened, Ford left the company bearing his name. Leland would go on to create the Cadillac automobile and Murphy renamed the company the Cadillac Automobile Company.

So, Henry Ford moved on once again. Teaming up with former racing cyclist Tom Cooper, Ford designed yet another automobile; this one the 80+ horsepower racer dubbed the "999." This contender would be driven by Barney Oldfield, who was a popular early twentieth-century driver. The 999 was navigated to victory in a race in October 1902.

Following his successes, Ford teamed up with one of his old friends, Alexander Y. Malcomson, who was a Detroit area coal dealer. They formed a partnership, Ford & Malcomson, Ltd., to make automobiles.

Ford wanted nothing more than to create and design a car for the people. This was what he set his mind to above all else. His next prototype would be affordable for the average person, yet a design which wouldn't be overlooked by the wealthy.

Ford and Malcomson found themselves a factory and went to work. For all of the parts that would be needed for his automobiles, Ford contracted with brothers John and Horace E. Dodge who owned a machine shop. They would supply Ford with over $160,000 in parts.

At first, sales were slow. With marketing not being what it is today, Ford and Malcomson were having a tough time moving their cars. To make matters worse, the Dodge brothers were soon on their doorstep looking for their money. This caused Ford a financial dilemma. Only quick thinking would save the day.

In response to the Dodge brothers request for payment, Malcomson brought in another group of investors and convinced the brothers to accept a portion of the new company. On June 16, 1903, Ford & Malcomson was reincorporated into the Ford Motor Company. The new investors had put up $28,000 in new capital and had saved the day.

Working to produce a newly designed car, Ford soon finished his masterpiece. It was driven on the ice-covered surface of Lake St. Clair, which lies between Michigan and Ontario. This vehicle was covering one mile in 39.4 seconds, and it set a new land-speed record going 91.3 miles per hour. Thanks to Barney Oldfield taking the car all around the country, people got to know the name of Henry Ford.

Ford not only loved designing and building his cars, but he also had a knack for racing them. In time, however, he would no longer be able to do this, as he was consumed with running his company. As time went by, Ford became rather dismissive of auto racing; he liked emphasizing the comfort and design of his new cars instead. He believed these vehicles had a higher purpose; to give people opportunities they would never have had otherwise. Even farming equipment was helped by Ford's designs, so racing was something that would eventually fall into the background of his interests.

Chapter Four

The Ford Motor Company and the Model T

"If you think you can do a thing or think you can't do a thing, you're right."

—Henry Ford

The beginning of the twentieth century in America was a vastly different place from what it is today. There was a definite distinction between those with money and those without. The automobile, as they were being created, was merely a plaything for the rich.

Most people couldn't drive any type of early automobile. They were complicated pieces of machinery, and if you were wealthy enough to afford one, you were wealthy enough to afford the chauffeur that went with it; someone who was very familiar with the inner workings of the vehicle. Henry Ford was determined that this automobile outlook should change. He wanted a car that was affordable to everyone—something simple enough that anyone could start the car and go.

Contrary to what some may believe, Ford did not invent the car. He was to produce an automobile that would be within the economic reach of most Americans. Most other car companies were happy to pander to the upper-class; probably believing in the long run, they would be the only ones with money enough to keep a car company going.

But what Henry Ford did was truly revolutionary. He created not only the Model T but the assembly line to go with it. This meant that over time, the price of his cars kept decreasing. Because of its design and method of manufacture, the Model T just kept dropping in price, making it remarkably affordable and tempting to own. And instead of pocketing the profits, Ford kept lowering the price of his car. As a result, Ford was to sell more cars and increase earnings in the Ford Motor Company than had ever happened before. He was the one responsible for transforming the luxury vehicle into the one used by the mainstay of American society.

The Model T was introduced on October 1, 1908. Its purchase price was $825. Breaking all records, the Model T sold over ten thousand copies in that first year. It had several distinctive features, like having the steering wheel on the left, which every other company soon copied. The entire engine and transmission were enclosed; there were four cylinders cast in a solid block, and two semi-elliptic springs were used for the suspension. Best of all, the car was easy to drive, simple to learn, and inexpensive to repair.

The price of the Model T kept dropping every year, and by 1912, the price was down to $575. Sales continued going strong, and by 1914 Ford would claim a 48% share of the automobile market. What car company can say that today?

Central to producing as many Model T's as he did, Ford couldn't have done it without the development of the assembly line. This was the key to increasing efficiency and keeping costs low. Ford was not the one who invented the assembly line, but he did perfect it. Before the assembly line as Ford created it, cars were individually built by teams of skilled workers. This process was slow and expensive. Ford was way ahead of the pack.

The assembly line reversed the process of automobile manufacture. No longer did the worker go to the car to work on it; now the car came to the worker, and each job was highly specialized, which the worker would repeat over and over. When the Model T was first assembled, it took over twelve hours to put one together. With the revised assembly line, the time to create one was reduced to under six hours.

The assembly line, as Ford envisioned it, was perfected in the years 1908-1913. Charles Sorensen, one of Ford's employees, was instrumental in making improvements to the method. In 1908 he recalled, "What was worked out at Ford was the practice of moving the work from one worker to another until it became a complete unit, then arranging the flow of those units at the right time and at the right place to a moving final assembly line from which came a finished product. Regardless of earlier uses of some of these principles, the direct line of succession of mass production and its intensification into automation stems directly from what we worked out at Ford Motor Company between 1908 and 1913 . . . As may be imagined, the job of putting the car together was a simpler one than handling the materials that had to be brought to it. Charlie Lewis, the youngest and most aggressive of our assembly foremen, and I tackled this problem. We gradually worked it out by bringing up only what we termed the fast-moving materials. The main bulky parts, like engines and axles, needed a lot of room. To give them that space, we left the smaller, more compact, light-handling material in a storage building on the northwest corner of the grounds. Then we arranged with the stock department to bring up at regular hours such divisions of material as we had marked out and packaged.

"This simplification of handling cleaned things up materially. But at best, I did not like it. It was then that the idea occurred to me that assembly would be easier, simpler and faster if we moved the chassis along, beginning at one end of the plant with a frame and adding the axles and the wheels; then moving it past the stockroom, instead of moving the stockroom to the chassis. I had Lewis arrange the materials on the floor so that what was needed at the start of assembly would be at that end of the building and the other parts would be along the line as we moved the chassis along. We spent every Sunday during July planning this. Then one Sunday morning, after the stock was laid out in this fashion, Lewis and I and a couple of helpers put together the first car, I'm sure that was ever built on a moving line."

In 1913, when the implementation of the assembly line was fine-tuned, a new plant in Highland Park was being built. When it was finished, assembly would begin on the top floor of the four-story building starting with the engine. Then the vehicle would move down floor by floor where finally the body was attached to the chassis.

This made a tremendous difference in the manufacture of the Model T. Along with his new car, Ford created a huge publicity arrangement in Detroit to ensure that the news about his new car would reach the public. Stories and ads were placed in every newspaper letting people know there was a car waiting for them.

Ford created a network of local dealers, and these helped to spread the word. Before long the Model T was the go-to car of the early twentieth century. Independent franchises were popping up all over the country, and these companies were becoming incredibly wealthy, all due to the Model T.

These car companies were not just advertising a new vehicle; what they were promoting was the concept of automobiling. New drivers began forming motor clubs, and more and more of the countryside was explored in your new Model T. As motor clubs grew, their members would meet on the weekends, and it was many a Sunday afternoon that one of those new-fangled cars would pass by villages and hamlets that had never seen anything like it. Conversation would ensue, the people living there would find out all about the Model T; how much it cost, where to buy one, how it ran and so on. Suddenly, smooth rides to far-away places were possible. The ripples that the Model T would create in society were enormous.

Ford never forgot the farmers, either. He believed his vehicle could be a real help to the modern farmer; it should be used as a commercial device to promote their business. As with sales for people in general, farm sales of the Model T skyrocketed.

The Model T was unlike any other invention of its time. Readily available for all people, what it did was to open up the country like never before. The Model T was the car that ran before there were good roads to run on. There were no interstate highways in America back then; only cow paths and horse trails, and dusty city roads that often turned to mud and muck over the seasons.

By 1913 Ford had introduced moving assembly belts into all of his plants. This made for an enormous increase in production. When his Model T was introduced in 1908, Ford was still interested in racing it. He created a special model racer, one with the lightest possible body and engine to run in a competition that stretched across the country. His car won the race, but only to be later disqualified.

Chapter Five

Ford's Expansion into Everyday Life

"You don't learn to walk by following rules. You learn by doing, and by falling over."

—Richard Branson

Being a pioneer of the automobile industry, Ford insisted on doing things the right way. He could have taken his vast wealth which was growing by leaps and bounds every year, and merely put the least amount of energy into his continued affairs. But, Henry Ford chose another way.

One of the things you got when you bought a car from the Ford Motor Company was a guarantee. Practically unknown in these days, Ford wanted people to see his company as one of service. Ford Service would come to mean that when you bought one of their cars, they should keep it running for you as long as possible at the lowest cost for upkeep.

In addition to keeping his customers happy, Ford was a great believer in "welfare capitalism." This concept first developed in the United States in the 1880s and was highly popular by the 1920s. Companies began to see that their workers were valuable members of society. In order to keep them, they started offering various programs and benefits to each employee.

Every company was different and benefits varied from place to place. Examples of welfare capitalism were company-sponsored sports teams, cafeteria plans, health care, lunchrooms, water fountains, company magazines, employee profit-sharing, and the start of retirement benefits.

Henry Ford was determined to improve the lot of his staff and wanted nothing more than to reduce the heavy turnover that saw many departments hiring 300 men per year to fill 100 slots. Once an employee was hired and trained, especially for a highly-specialized assembly line, the last thing you wanted him or her to do was to go elsewhere for work.

In 1914, Ford astonished the world by introducing a $5 per day wage. This would be equivalent to $120 today, quite an extraordinary venture for the time. This more than doubled the rate of most of the workers and was a real boon to the team of the Ford Motor Company. Most employees were a part of the assembly-line system and found this type of work to be rather boring as the hours went by. But, when Ford implemented qualified workers $5 a day, the upsides far overshadowed the monotony of the tasks.

A $5 a day wage was twice the rate of what most Americans were making at the time. Some business owners questioned Ford's motives; even believing he was a socialist. The day the doors were opened for applications, more than 10,000 men had lined up at the Highland Park factory to be hired.

The best mechanics in Detroit flocked to the Ford Motor Company. Ford's $5 a day wage went into effect on January 5, 1914, raising everyone's pay from $2.34. Even though Detroit was a high-wage city, this forced all other companies in competition with Henry Ford to also raise their prices or lose their best team members.

Now Ford employees could also buy Ford cars. This raised their self-esteem and did wonders for efficiency at work. Workers knew they would be rewarded based on their good character and how productive they were. Once you were at Ford Motor Company for longer than six months, you could participate in profit-sharing. This was based upon certain rules that Ford himself set down. The company looked down on heavy drinking, gambling, and what we call today, deadbeat dads. Ford set up a Social Department which oversaw every employee closely.

By today's standards, it would seem as if Henry Ford was intruding on his workers' private lives. Having the company's Social Department overseeing your home life would seem a great injustice to people in the twenty-first century. Yet Ford really believed in his worker's characters. He thought that idle time led to idle endeavors, many of which were money-wasters.

Once the $5 a day wage went into effect, Ford and his company watched how their men spent their money. Some used their spare time to take on extra jobs, some invested their money, and some men squandered their pay. Some even lived the way they always lived and put the surplus in the bank. Over time, less supervision was needed as workers adjusted themselves to what a living wage and lifestyle meant to them.

Not everyone agreed with Ford's decision to raise wages. The Dodge Brothers, for instance, sued Ford Motor Company demanding that they release more of the company's profits to shareholders instead of reinvesting them.

One thing that was growing larger every day in America in the early years of the twentieth century was the middle class. More and more accouterments, everything from hairdressers to electricity, were available for the general population. Now, people could boast that they were also automobile owners.

Sales of Ford's Model T were exploding. They were over 250,000 in 1914, and the basic touring car price soon dropped to a remarkable $360. When this happened in 1916, sales went to 472,000. All of the cars were painted black because black was the color that dried the fastest on the assembly line. Ford was famous for quipping, "Any customer can have a car painted any color that he wants so long as it is black." You could, if you so desired, have your acquisition in red or another color, but that was a custom order, and it would cost more money. Most people were happy to have the car in black.

When World War I erupted, Henry Ford opposed it, seeing it as a colossal waste. Ford became one of the country's most outspoken public figure to disapprove of the war. He stayed far away from people who were profiting from it.

In 1915, Ford along with other pacifists were determined to do something about ending the fighting. Because of his vast wealth, Ford had another home in Fort Myers, Florida, right next door to his good friend Thomas Edison. One of the people whom Ford had invited to his home there, was the Hungarian-born Jewish pacifist and feminist, Rosika Schwimmer. Together, they agreed to fund a "Peace Ship" and head to Europe. Ford and 170 prominent peace leaders traveled to the Netherlands and then to Sweden. Even his own pastor, Reverend Samuel Marquis, went along for the ride. President Wilson didn't give this mission any support, but that didn't stop the voyage. Unfortunately, the ship was a target of great ridicule, and once it reached Sweden, Ford left it and returned home.

It was around this time that Henry Ford's anti-Semitism began to raise its ugly head. Before the ship embarked for Europe, Ford had told Rosika Schwimmer that "I know who caused the war—the German-Jewish bankers. I have the evidence here." And he deftly patted his jacket pocket.

He declared he had facts which he couldn't reveal at the time because he didn't have them all.

Early in the war, Ford's factories in Britain were producing tractors to increase the British food supply, but eventually, they were used for making trucks and aircraft engines. When the U.S. entered the war in 1917, all factories became major suppliers of weapons, especially the Liberty engine for airplanes and anti-submarine boats. Ford's plants were not spared.

By 1918 with the war still going, President Woodrow Wilson encouraged Ford to run for the Senate seat in Michigan. Wilson was advocating for his League of Nations, which he formed as the war was winding down. The League was to be an intergovernmental organization, one that would put an end to all future wars.

If Henry Ford ran and won in Michigan, Wilson believed that could tip the scales in Congress in favor of the League. The president wrote to Ford, "You are the only man in Michigan who can be elected and help bring about the peace you so desire."

Ford then wrote back to the president, "If they want to elect me let them do so, but I won't make a penny's investment." Ford was on the ballot that year and came within 4,500 votes of actually winning the seat. Nevertheless, he remained in Wilson's corner and was always a supporter of the League of Nations.

Once the war ended in November 1918, it was just one month later that Henry Ford turned over control of the Ford Motor Company to his son Edsel. He still retained the right to veto anything he didn't like, and there were sometimes disagreements between father and son.

In the meantime, Ford started another company, Henry Ford and Son, where he made it known in influential circles that he was taking not only himself but all of his best employees to his new company. Ford was attempting to scare the remaining holdout stockholders of the Ford Motor Company into selling their shares to him before they lost value.

Together with Edsel, Henry Ford began buying up the company's stock. The ruse worked, and father and son soon became sole owners of their business. In 1919 when the Dodge brothers had won their lawsuit against the Ford Motor Company, neither one was able to enjoy their victory. John Dodge succumbed to the influenza epidemic that swept over the globe after World War I, and his brother Horace died of cirrhosis that same year.

Ford's private secretary Ernest Liebold had, in 1918, purchased a little-known weekly newspaper *The Dearborn Independent* which ran for the next eight years. Every Ford factory carried the paper and gave it out to all employees. This marked the start of the decade where Ford emerged as a "respected spokesmen for right-wing extremism and religious prejudice."

Once the Great War was just a memory, Ford set his sights on making his company internationally known. Ford's philosophy was one of economic independence for the United States. He truly believed there was no better place to be the leader in world production of goods and services, as well as in world finance. The new plant at River Rouge, located in Dearborn, Michigan, became the world's largest industrial complex.

One of Ford's dreams had been to build his cars "from scratch." This meant that he could pursue what is known as "vertical integration," an arrangement in which the supply of a company is owned by that company. Andrew Carnegie had used this method in the nineteenth century, and many other business moguls had followed suit.

Vertical integration meant that Ford's River Rouge plant could manufacture their own steel. This spoke directly to Ford's vision for his company; that cars could be produced entirely from scratch without reliance on foreign trade.

Ford was a great advocate of the global expansion of his business. He also believed that international trade and cooperation between nations would lead to global peace. He surmised that one of the best ways to demonstrate this was through his assembly-line factories being set up all over the industrial world.

Assembly plants had opened in Britain and Canada as early as 1911, and the following year Ford had cooperated with Giovanni Agnelli of Fiat to begin the first plants in Italy. In the 1920s, the first plants were built in Germany with the encouragement of President Herbert Hoover and the Commerce Department. True to his word, Henry Ford continued opening plants in Australia, India, and France. By 1929, Ford had successful dealerships on all six continents.

Chapter Six
Ventures in Later Life

"If you can't make it good, at least make it look good."

—Bill Gates

In 1929 it was relatively easy to provide technical aid to the Soviet Government in building the first Soviet automobile plant. The technical assistance agreement had been concluded for nine years and had been signed in Dearborn, Michigan by Henry Ford on May 31.

This contract involved the purchase of $30,000,000 worth of knocked-down Ford trucks and cars for assembly for the first four years of the plant's operation. After the four years, the plant would start to switch over to Soviet-made components.

Ford sent his best technicians and engineers to the Soviet Union to help train the working staff and assist with installing the equipment. One of those crackerjack tool and die makers was none other than Walter Reuther, who had joined the Ford Motor Company in 1927. His socialist leanings and his union career would become one of Ford's worst nightmares in the 1930s.

In Detroit and Dearborn, there were over one hundred Soviet engineers and technicians learning the processes of manufacture and assembly in the company's plants. Ford was quoted as saying, "No matter where industry prospers, whether in India or China, or Russia, the more profit there will be for everyone, including us. All the world is bound to catch some good from it."

Way back in 1903, the Ford Motor Company had debuted its first automobile, the Model A. This original car came with a price tag of $800 to $900. It came as a two-seater runabout, a popular version of early cars, which meant it had no windshield, top, or doors. It was a well-liked car up until 1915. There was also a "tonneau" model, which was a hard or a soft cover used to protect the passenger seats and could be removed. There is an old song from the Broadway musical Oklahoma which is titled "The Surrey With The Fringe On Top." That would be a Model A.

This version of the Model A only lasted from 1903-1904. Even though Ford advertised the Model A as the "most reliable machine in the world," it suffered many problems which were common to all early automobiles. Things like overheating and slipping transmission bands were regularly causing the car to break down. Of course, if you were stuck on the side of the road, you were sure to be seen in your shiny red car, as that was the color of all Model A's.

By 1926, believe it or not, the Model T wasn't doing so well. Competitors, especially those from the various General Motors divisions were catching up to Ford's numbers with all the cars they were now selling. In fact, some of these divisions offered more powerful engines, convenience features, and cosmetic customizations.

When Ford executives brought this revelation to Ford himself, he didn't act on the news at first. Before long he came to realize that perhaps a new model car would be the answer. In October 1927, the first new Model A's rolled off the assembly line. This new Model A was the go-to car for 1928, even coming in four standard colors.

Body styles for the Model A included the Tudor at $500, available in gray, green, or black, and the Town Car for $1200, which was top of the line. Top speed was around 65 miles per hour.

The Model A came in many different styles, including a Coupe, Business Coupe, Sports Coupe, Roadster Coupe, Convertible Cabriolet, Convertible Sedan, Phaeton, Tudor Sedan, Town Car, Fordor 2-window, Fordor 3-window, Victoria, Station Wagon, Taxicab, Truck, and Commercial.

The Model A was the second fabulously successful automobile that was launched by the Ford Motor Company. It was produced through 1931 with total sales exceeding four million. It wasn't until the 1930s that Ford finally relented about his objection to finance companies, and the Ford-owned Universal Credit Corporation came into existence.

By 1932, one-third of all vehicles in the world were produced by the Ford Motor Company. Henry Ford's expansion into all corners of the globe was not just a financial decision on his part. He believed that by introducing the world to hard work and productivity, it would remain free from strife, especially the kind that led to war.

Henry Ford's Model A was so popular that it was even memorialized in song. Composer Irving Kaufman wrote a melody called "Henry's Made a Lady Out of Lizzie" which referenced the "Tin Lizzie," a nickname which had once been given to the Model T. Another big seller were model car kits. Young and old can still to this day put together one of Henry Ford's remarkable vehicles.

As if creating and manufacturing cars wasn't enough for Ford, he became fascinated with airplanes. During World War I, Ford's company had built Liberty engines for the aviation business, and this was something that Ford took a liking to. Of course, he returned to manufacturing his cars, but in 1925 he acquired the Stout Metal Airplane Company.

So it was that Henry Ford began building airplanes. The most successful of Ford's aircrafts was the Ford 4AT Trimotor, most often referred to as the "Tin Goose" because it was constructed of corrugated metal. The Trimotor first flew on June 11, 1926, and was the first successful passenger airliner. Twelve passengers could—quite uncomfortably—be accommodated. Almost 200 Trimotors were built before production stopped in 1933, due to the onset of the Great Depression. The Ford Airplane Division was shut down at that time because of poor sales.

Chapter Seven

Disdain of Labor Unions

"All honor's wounds are self-inflicted."

—Andrew Carnegie

If there was one thing that Henry Ford hated worse than anything else, it was labor unions. He felt that unions were always controlled by those who ran them, and despite some of their noble motives, most often labor unions ended up doing more harm than good to its workers.

Henry Ford paid his staff well. He was the one who had doubled their salaries, introduced a five-day workweek, and wanted his sound rules of living to rub off on his employees. Following his vision of improving the lives of his employees, Ford saw no use for labor unions in any of his companies.

Unions were notorious for limiting production as a way to foster employment; why have one person doing a job when you can split the work and employ three people? As a contrast, according to Ford's business philosophy, the only way to success was through high productivity. Ford thought of his workers as an extended family, so why would he want something to come along, that he suspected wouldn't be good for them?

Ford believed that union leaders had the job of stirring up bad blood between management and employees in any company. They were using the socio-economic view of things never being "fair" to foment violence. This view also helped the union leaders to maintain their own power. Ford acknowledged there were good and bad managers in any company; the trick was to weed out the bad and replace them with the good. This way, those same smart managers would do right by their workers, which, in turn, would maximize profits. It wasn't rocket science.

To keep unions at bay, Ford promoted Harry Bennett, a former Navy boxer, to head the Service Department. Bennett started implementing tactics which went a long way in squashing down union organizing. The most famous incident took place on May 26, 1937, at the River Rouge Plant complex. Bennett's security men beat United Auto Workers representatives with clubs. One of those involved with the UAW was Walter Reuther. While Bennett's men were beating the UAW reps, the police chief on the scene, one Carl Brooks who had worked for Bennett's Service Department, refused to give the order to intervene. This violent scene became known as The Battle of the Overpass.

Unfortunately for Ford, this event greatly increased support for the UAW and hurt Ford's reputation. By the late 1930s and into the 1940s, Edsel, who was now president of the Ford Motor Company, believed that the company had to come to some sort of agreement with the unions. At this point, there were work disruptions, violence, and bitter stalemates and Edsel recognized that this kind of behavior could not go on any longer.

There needed to be a collective bargaining agreement. Collective bargaining is a process of negotiation between employers and a group of employees where both sit down and hammer out agreements for working salaries, conditions, compensation, and other worker rights.

Henry Ford who still had the final veto on all things to do with his company refused to cooperate. For the next few years, Harry Bennett kept talking to the unions that were trying to unionize the Ford Motor Company. Ford believed that by talking to the unions, no union agreements could ever be put in place.

Whether Henry Ford thought the unions would just go away if enough time passed is not known. The Ford Motor Company was the last Detroit automaker to recognize the United Auto Workers union (UAW). In April 1941, a sit-down strike was called by the union which closed the River Rouge plant. A distraught Henry Ford threatened to shut down his entire business, and he came very near to following through on his ultimatum. Only the fact that his wife Clara told him she would leave him if he destroyed the family business, brought him to his senses.

It seemed as if overnight the Ford Motor Company went from being a stubborn union hold-out to being a company with one of the most favorable UAW contract terms. The union contract was signed in June 1941.

Chapter Eight

The Anti-Semite Problem

"We don't want tradition. We want to live in the present and the only history that is worth a tinker's damn is the history we make today."

—Henry Ford

In the years between 1910 and 1918, Henry Ford became increasingly anti-immigrant, anti-labor, anti-liquor, and anti-Semitic. He wanted to let the world know his views on just about everything; after all, he was an inventor and a tycoon and knew better than the average Joe. One of the things Ford wanted people to know was that there was a Jewish conspiracy to control the world.

Once Henry Ford had his *Dearborn Independent* newspaper running regularly he began writing anti-Semitic articles. In Germany, these articles were published in four volumes, all under the title "The International Jew."

Paradoxically, by the early 1920s, Ford had a reputation for actively seeking out and hiring black workers. He wasn't accused of Jewish discrimination or of not dealing with Jewish suppliers. But he did intend to use his newly acquired newspaper as his public mouthpiece. Ford had practical ideas that he wanted to give to the public.

Ford addressed his newspaper to the common people. Two-thirds of those reading the *Dearborn Independent* lived in small towns or in the countryside. They looked with great affection on Henry Ford. He knew these were the "real" Americans and he was out to teach them his truth about the world.

The recent war, the Russian Revolution, the modernization of America and the economic slump were all things putting American life in jeopardy. Ford was convinced that all of these events were traceable to one source, and he was going to tell the nation what that was.

By the 1920s, Ford positioned E.G. Pipp as editor for his *Independent*. Pipp had known Ford a few years before going to work for him, and it was in the ensuing years that he began to notice a change in Ford. Ford was "bringing up the Jews frequently, almost continuously in conversation, blaming them for almost everything." Ford asserted it was the Jewish international financiers who were behind all war. In May 1920, the front page of Ford's newspaper declared, "The International Jew: The World's Problem." This was the first of 91 articles that would appear consecutively. Pipp resigned in disgust when the first article appeared.

A few months after these articles started to pop up, certain people around Ford introduced him to a Russian émigré, Paquita de Shishmareff. She had with her a copy of *The Protocols of the Elders of Zion*, now known as an evil forgery created by the Russian czar's secret service at the turn of the century. In it were a series of lectures by a Jewish elder giving a complete run-down on how European governments were to be overthrown.

Ford's articles were denounced by the Anti-Defamation League (ADL), and while the texts condemned pogroms and violence against Jews, they blamed Jews for provoking incidents of violence. The columns had been relegated to Ford's second editor, William Cameron, to write, but they were all heartily endorsed by Henry Ford.

For seven years the *Dearborn Independent* continued running these stories until finally a California farm cooperative organizer, Aaron Sapiro, sued Ford for libel. Others had sued before, but Sapiro was the first one to get a trial. Ford wouldn't testify and may have even staged an automobile accident so he could go to the hospital instead. The judge declared a mistrial and Ford settled out of court. Jewish leaders had called for a boycott of his cars, and slumping sales may have motivated Ford to settle.

Louis Marshall, chairman of the American Jewish Committee, brokered an agreement whereby Ford announced that any articles reflective of the Jews would never appear in his newspaper again. Ford was "mortified" to learn that *The Protocols of the Elders of Zion* were fake; he even offered Jews his "future friendship and goodwill." In December 1927, the *Independent* was closed for good.

Interestingly, the German Ford plants in Cologne and Berlin both utilized slave labor during the war. One of the workers, Elsa Iwanowa, was taken from Russia by the Germans when she was 16. "They put us on barracks on 3-tier bunks. It was very cold they did not pay us at all and scarcely fed us. The only reason that we survived is that we were young and fit."

It was unclear how much contact Ford's Dearborn facilities had with Germany after 1941. They claim they were completely cut off. There has been speculation yet nothing has been proven. After the war, Ford sued the U.S. Government for wartime damages in which his German facilities had been destroyed due to Allied bombings. He receives almost one million dollars, mostly for damage done to a military truck complex in Cologne.

Chapter Nine
Later Years and Death

"If you never want to be criticized, for goodness' sake don't do anything new."

—Jeff Bezos

Henry Ford was vehemently opposed to the U.S. entering World War II. He had accused Jews of stirring up aggressions which had led to the First World War, and he believed the same thing was happening again. Ford continued to do business with Nazi Germany, including the manufacture of war materiel. He did line up behind the war effort when war was declared in December 1941.

Once America was in the war, Ford directed that a new factory at Willow Run near Detroit, be built. Ground was broken there in 1942, and the first B-24 came off the line in October. Being the largest assembly-line in the world at the time, the Willow Run plant produced 650 B-24s every month.

In May 1943, tragedy struck the Ford family. Edsel Ford had developed stomach cancer, and no treatment or surgery was successful. The cancer spread and at the age of 49, Edsel died. This meant that the ailing and aging Henry Ford once again resumed the presidency of the company. At this point in his life, Henry had already had several heart attacks and strokes, and his mental abilities were starting to weaken.

Most of the board of directors did not want Ford as president. But Ford had always enjoyed having some kind of input in his company during years he was not formally running it and now was no different. Ford chose to serve as president until the end of the war.

In September 1945, with World War II officially over, Ford gave over the company presidency to his grandson Henry Ford II. He then went into retirement. On April 7, 1947, Henry Ford died of a cerebral hemorrhage at his estate in Dearborn. He was 83 years old.

Funeral services were held at Detroit's Cathedral Church of St. Paul, and he was buried in the Ford cemetery in Detroit.

Chapter Ten

Henry Ford's Legacy

"Failure is only the opportunity to begin again, only this time more wisely."

—Henry Ford

What is one to make of Henry Ford? He certainly was an American success story; just another farm boy who left rural America to make his mark in the world. He didn't invent the horseless carriage, but he brought an affordable, well-run car to the masses. His automobile helped to transform the nation.

Living in a post-modern age, where it has all been done for us, it's easy to lose sight of how revolutionary these inventions actually were. Picture a town without cars, with dirt paths for roads, spotty electricity, and a single phone down at the general store. This was the world of the young Henry Ford. And if you wanted to get somewhere, you either walked or rode a horse. Ford had yet to use that "horsepower" to rein in his vehicles.

Ford may have been the first car company, but he helped to create all the rest; Dodge, Cadillac, General Motors, Audi, Mercedes, Jaguar, Toyota, Kia, and tomorrow there will be a new one. Ford wasn't happy with just one model; he kept introducing new ones, and better engines for commercial vehicles, too.

Ford was wise enough to appreciate his workers to the point of giving them a good living wage and a 5-day workweek. No one, up to this point, cared too much to do such a thing. And in his "wisdom" Henry Ford believed that he knew best. Sometimes, what you achieve is enough. Unfortunately for Ford, he allowed sentiments which today would drive him right out of business to become the centerpiece of his business.

Henry Ford never understood or appreciated his only acknowledged son, Edsel. It is said that he hounded him to death. Where the young Edsel wanted to introduce different colors and more convenience into their cars, he was constantly bullied by his father. Yet, Henry never got over his son's death. After Edsel's death, Henry was often seen wandering the roads around Greenfield Village at night.

One hundred thousand people showed up for the funeral. Henry Ford meant something to them, and every time you put your car in drive, he should mean something to you, too. He was a true visionary who wanted more for the common man. There were honors and awards given to Ford, the same as other movers of society; his life was meaningful, and it is highly likely that America was transformed by what he brought to it.

He not only figured out a new way of making his cars, but his assembly-line philosophy would also carry over into the wars he so adamantly opposed. Nowhere close to the amount of material produced could have been achieved, had it not been for his insight.

Would someone else have come along? Could another industrialist have done the same? We'll never know because history had a place reserved for Henry Ford. For the most part, he played his part well.

Conclusion

Mention the Model T, and most people will come to think of Henry Ford. His was the first automobile to be mass-produced, and it was done on the assembly line he invented. His low-cost, reliable cars were what put most ordinary Americans in the driver's seat at the turn of the twentieth century.

But Henry Ford's legacy rides on more than just mere wheels. His company, the Ford Motor Company, is still with us today, over a hundred years after it was established. It survived two world wars and some dark moments when Henry Ford was trying to connect his ideas to the world's, but it has lasted as a monument to the man who started it.

Henry Ford is probably the man, above any other of the twentieth century, who turned the working class into the middle class. Most Americans enjoy an unprecedented middle-class existence, owning most amenities they can imagine. That is due to the manufacturing industry which had its start with Henry Ford. From cars to engines to roads to shopping centers to war equipment, it has all been mass-produced.

Today, if you love NFL football, you can catch a game by the Detroit Lions at Ford Field. In Dearborn, there is the Ford Community and Performing Arts Center, Henry Ford Retirement Village and the Ford Homes District. You can get there on Interstate 94 from Detroit. It's called the Ford Freeway, and that is no coincidence.

Printed in Great Britain
by Amazon